Romantic Valentines

By Dan & Pauline Campanelli

D1558851

ISBN#: 0-89538-078-1

Published by: L-W Book Sales
P.O. Box 69
Gas City, IN 46933

Please write for our free catalog.

NOTE REGARDING PRICES:

This is a price guide, and as such they are not fixed values and should be regarded as reference only. Neither the authors nor the publisher can be held responsible for any gains or losses incurred as a result of consulting this guide.

Printed by IMAGE GRAPHICS, INC., Paducah, Kentucky

INTRODUCTION

Here at our home at Flying Witch Farm, when all the treasured ornaments of Yuletide have been taken down and packed away for another year, when the warmth and joy of the holiday season are behind us and only the cold white days of winter lie ahead, it is the time to decorate the house with our collection of antique valentines, to warm our hearts and celebrate the holiday of LOVE. We began collecting valentines almost two decades ago, when one bleak February day a friend sent us an antique valentine as a Valentine's Day card, a beautiful lithograph of Cupid himself, lighting the Olympic torch of love atop a column of honeycomb tissue. We had just begun collecting Halloween at the time and every now and then the delicate snowflake beauty of a paper lace valentine or the exquisite forget-me-nots of a fabulous pull-out would catch our eye, and soon we began collecting valentines as well.

Unlike Halloween items (see our book "*Halloween Collectables*", L-W Books, Gas City, IN) which were made to be discarded, valentines were kept and treasured down through the years. They were often saved and kept in scrapbooks, and today it is possible to find entire collections, or scrapbooks still intact, or to find a large number of early valentines all addressed to the same person.

A valentine is defined by Webster's as "a card containing a profession of love, sent on St. Valentines Day, February 14th".

When we think of valentines today we tend to think of the lovely lacy creations covered with violets and rosebuds that were given to ladies of Victorian days, but the holiday itself has much more ancient roots. According to legend, Valentine's Day is celebrated in honor of St. Valentinus, a Christian who was martyred by Emperor Claudius II for insulting the pagan gods of Rome. It is said that he created the first valentine when he pricked the message "Remember me, your valentine" on the heart shaped leaf of a violet, just before he died on Feb. 14, 271 C.E. (current era). But Feb. 15th was a holy day in Rome and throughout the ancient world, which predates Christianity by many centuries. *Lupercalia*, as it was called, was a celebration of love and the return of fertility. The priests of Dionysus, the *Luperci*, ran about the streets of the cities striking barren women

3

on the palms with leather tongs in order to restore fertility, and young men chose their female partners for the day's festivities by drawing lots.

The grade school Valentine's Day party, at which children dropped valentines into elaborately decorated boxes to be selected at random by other children, seems to be an ancient echo of the Lupercalia. Even the flowers and symbols with which valentines have been decorated have their roots in the ancient past. The heart, the very symbol of Valentine's Day, was believed by the ancient Greeks and Romans to be the organ which was the seat of romantic love. Doves were sacred to Aphrodite (the Greek counterpart of Venus, the Roman goddess of love and beauty) and Cupid (whom the Greeks called Eros), who is usually depicted as a winged cherub with a quiver of arrows and is none other than the son of Venus.

The custom of exchanging tokens or messages of love at mid-February is believed to have originated in Italy, and probably has its roots in these earlier Roman celebrations. It survived the plagues and persecutions of the Middle Ages and by the 14th century had spread to England where it took root. Margery Bowes is credited with sending the "first" valentine when, in 1471, she wrote to her cousin saying "Friday is St. Valentine's Day, and every bird chases a mate". In Europe, by the mid-18th century, valentines were being commercially produced, while here in the New World they were being made by hand. In the early 1800's in England, Dobbs and Co. was producing cards on a major scale. In Massachusetts, Esther Howland is said to have produced 100,000 cards a year by the 1860's.

The delicate snowflake beauty of the paper lace creations such as those by Howland, George Whitney and others continued, and by the turn of the century had been joined by intricate diecut and embossed pull-outs printed mostly in Germany in beautiful chromolithography. To this was added the wonderful invention of meshed, or honeycomb tissue, which could be cut into a variety of shapes for stunning effects. Meshed tissue began in Europe, but the Beistle Co. of Shippensburg, PA., patented a process for making it and soon produced their own line of distinctive valentines. Penny post cards, just as flowery and romantic as their paper lace cousins were produced by the thousands from the turn of the century to around World War I. The standard folder, similar to today's greeting cards, were being made as well, but from the mid-1800's valentines seemed to become more and more lavish, and probably reached a peak around 1900. After World War I, valentines gradually became simpler, less embossed, "cuter". They also became smaller, and there was a trend toward mechanical cards with moving parts.

With all these styles and types of valentines it isn't always easy to date one precisely, unless it was dated by the original sender. An enormous number of valentines were printed in Germany, and about 1930, the U.S. government required that products being imported into this country be marked "Made in (country of origin)". One may occasionally find a card marked "Made in Germany" signed and dated earlier, but that is the exception. Generally, valentines simply marked "Germany" are earlier than 1930. Those marked "Printed in Germany", however, may date as early as the late 1800's, the German lithographers being rightfully proud of their craft.

Of course post cards, if they have been sent to someone, are dated by the U.S. government, and many valentines were dated by their senders. Dated valentines and post cards not only date themselves, but are clues to dating other valentines that are similar in style or technique. One thing that does not help date a valentine is clothing style. 18th century and Elizabethan costumes were very popular subjects on Victorian valentines. Methods of transportation however are excellent clues to dating. Automobiles became popular on valentines right after the turn of the century. Airplanes and dirigibles were very popular in the 1930's, but dirigibles probably lost popularity after the Hindenburg disaster.

Whether a valentine can be dated to the mid-1800's or to the years just prior to World War II, we have to respect it for its age as well as its beauty, and do all we can to preserve it for future generations. Valentines, like all antique paper, should be stored in a dry, dust-free environment, away from paper eating insects. Honeycomb tissue should be carefully refolded and held with a paper clip. Antique paper should never be wrapped in paper unless it is acid-free. We keep our valentines in plastic bags so they can be handled and admired without being damaged. Damage, however, is inevitable as old paper is very brittle. If damage does occur, cellophane tape should never be used. Instead, a bit of acid-free paper with white glue can be used to attach parts that have broken off.

The valentines on the following pages are from our own collection unless otherwise noted, and we enjoy sharing their very special beauty with others. This book is also a price guide, and the prices given are for items that are in "good" condition. While some price guides give values for a single object ranging from $5 to $500, such "ballpark" values render a price guide useless. The prices given here are neither flea market nor auction house prices, but the current retail value that we have paid for these or similar pieces at antique shops.

Every year, on about the 2nd of February, whether or not the ground hog sees his shadow, Dan and I perform a certain ritual. We open the trunk in which our collection of antique valentines is stored. One at a time we remove them, the exquisite paper lace, the intricate pull-outs, the honeycomb tissue, the cherubs and violets and forget-me-nots. We admire and unwrap them, and then we decorate the entire house with them, every mantle and shelf, every desk top and high-boy and cubboard. We gaze at their beauty and then we go out in search of more. Dan and I have made it a tradition to buy one another antique valentines every year rather than buying new cards at the mall. And, for a few weeks our home is filled with the beauty and the romance of these wonderful works of art.

Dan & Pauline Campanelli
Flying Witch Farm

TABLE OF CONTENTS

ACKNOWLEDGMENTS

Kimberly Baker
Julia Bartels - River Run Antiques
Sue & Candy at C.P.I.
Patrick Campbell
Charles Gottschall
Kim Kurki
Morris Museum
Harry & Darlene Newman
Gail Reuben and Family

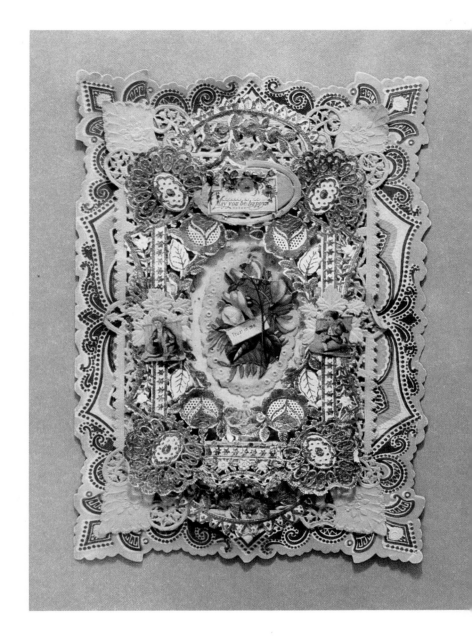

Here is a perfect example of a Victorian valentine. It has two layers of paper lace, separated by folded paper hinges to give it depth. One layer of lace is guilded, and the flowers on the chromolithographed scrap in the center are sweet peas, meaning "delicate pleasures". Late 1800's, 5 1/2" x 7 1/2" **$55+**

Paper Lace

CHAPTER 1

When we think of antique valentines, the majority of us probably visualize the paper lace masterpieces made by people like Esther Howland. In 1849, in Worchester, Massachusetts, Esther Howland started the New England Valentine Company. Here, she and a group of women, using an assembly line system, are said to have produced 100,000 cards a year by 1860. These cards were assembled by hand of some of the most exquisite paper lace and chromolithographed "scraps" produced in Europe and selected by Howland. One of her trademarks was the accordion-folded paper hinges that lifted the paper lace away from the card itself, giving the valentine a more dimensional look. Glazed paper wafers were employed in a similar way. Her cards can sometimes be identified by the small initial "H" on the card itself or on a tiny label on the card, or by the initials "N.E.V. Co." printed on cards of the 1870's.

Although it is usually said the Esther Howland employees were women, at least one exception was George Whitney, who in 1866 started his own company. He produced valentines almost identical in style to those made by Howland. Whitney bought the New England Valentine Company from Howland in 1880, when her father became ill and required her full time attention. Whitney's cards were sometimes signed with a small "W", later they were marked "Whitney Made". The Whitney Card Co. continued producing valentines until World War II.

At the same time that Howland and Whitney were producing cards, young ladies in this country were encouraged to produce handmade ones, and in Europe cards were being made by such manufacturers as Dobbs & Co. and Louis Prang.

The typical anatomy of a paper lace valentine begins with a folded card printed with a lacy design on the front. Upon this is mounted a small printed central design, around which are one or two layers of die cut lace. One of these layers may be hand gilded or of gold or silver Dresden. The layers may be separated by folded paper hinges, or have colored wafers of paper behind them to accent a particularly lovely part of the paper lace. Inside, the card might have a printed sentiment, or one that has been pasted in, or a lady might insert her own calling card.

The lovely portrait of the young lady on this exquisite gift box (above) is surrounded by Dresden borders. The box still contains the original paper lace valentine. The center of the valentine opens to reveal a message. Dated 1889, 7 1/2" x 7 1/2" card with box   **$95+**

This lovely valentine (below) has silver lace Dresden surrounding a winter landscape. Last quarter 19th Century, 6" x 9"   **$65+**

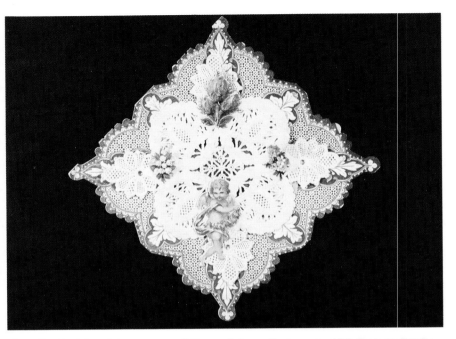

The valentine (above) has an unusual diamond shape. Last quarter 19th Century, 5 1/2" x 5 1/2".   **$35+**

The valentine (below) has a very unusual paper lace design. Last quarter 19th Century, 6 3/4" x 6 3/4".   **$35+**

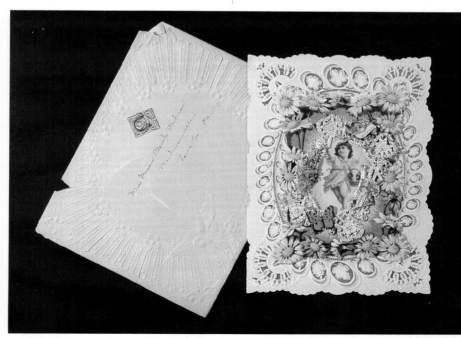

12

It is rare to find an early valentine with its original envelope. The two valentines on the opposite page both have exquisitely embossed envelopes and were apparently sent to a sister and brother. Unfortunately, the post mark is illegible. Late 1800's, 5 1/2" x 7 1/2", card with envelope   **$55+ each**

The lovely valentine (above) is probably made by Whitney, as are the ones opposite. Late 1800's, 6" x 8"   **$45+**

The two exquisite cards on the opposite page are beautiful examples of chromolithography and the lace is hand cut on both. Last half 19th Century, 7" x 7" **$65+ each**

Here (right) is another example of a card typical of the kind made by Esther Howland. Mid- late 1800's, 6 1/2" x 9"   **$50+**

Valentines like this one (below) obviously date before the rate for over-sized postage! Mid- late 1800's, 11" x 11"   **$95+**

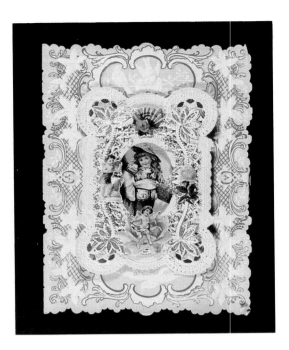

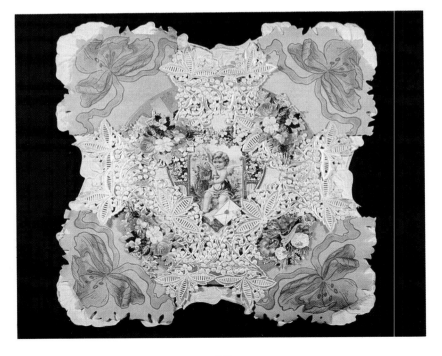

The three tiny valentines on the opposite page all have exquisite lace and finely embossed cards. The valentine on the bottom is marked Whitney. Mid-1800's, 3" x 5"   **$35+ each**

Both of the valentines on this page have very fine paper lace. The upper one has lace that has been hand guilded, and it also has red paper wafers under the lace. Mid- late 1800's, 4 1/2" x 6" **$45+ each**

Here (left) is another example of unusual paper lace on a card printed with apple blossoms, meaning "preference". Late 1800's, 6 1/2" x 4 1/2" **$35+**

Both cards below employ paper hinges to give the paper lace an extra dimension. Late 1800's, 6 1/2" x 4 1/2" **$35+ each**

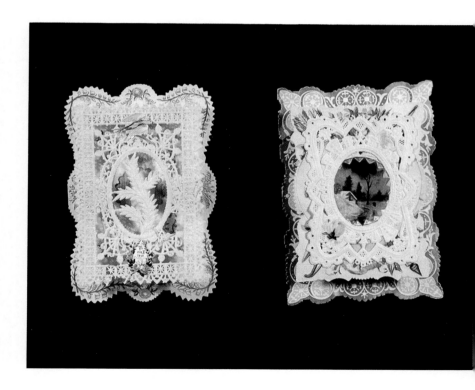

The valentine below has a lovely silver Dresden scrap below the central motif. Last quarter 19th century, 4 1/2" x 6" **$25+**

The valentines right and bottom right both have the same printed background, but one is printed in blue, the other in pink. Ca. 1880's, 4 1/2" x 6" **$25+ each**

Exquisite silver Dresden frames Cupid on a bicycle on this lovely valentine at left. Last quarter 19th Century, 5 1/2" x 7 1/2"   **$45+**

Below, paper lace, gold Dresden and scraps frame a couple on one card, while two white paper lace hearts open to reveal a lovely landscape on the other. Last quarter 19th Century, 5 1/2" x 8" **$35+ each**

White lace and silver Dresden frame a tiny landscape on this handsome valentine (right). Last quarter 19th Century, 5 1/2" x 7 1/2" **$45+**

The two small valentines below employ paper hinges. The card on the right has gold Dresden lace. Late 1800's, 4 1/2" x 5 1/2" **$35+ each**

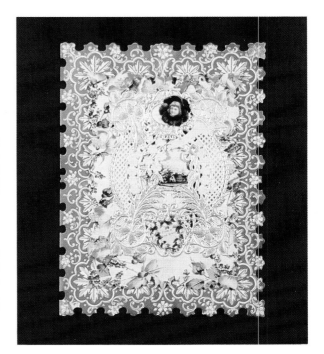

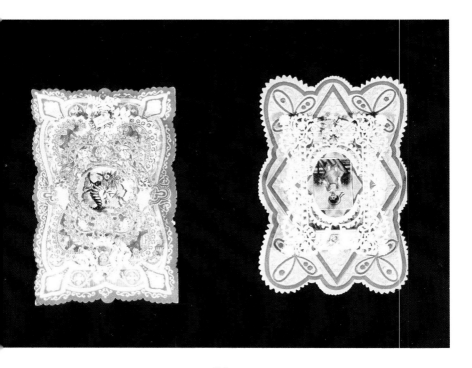

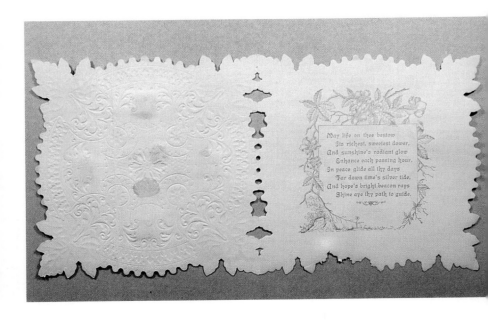

By looking at the insides of these lovely cards from the late 1800's it is possible to appreciate the fine embossing which, on the front of the cards, is often disguised by the printed design. The card above shows stains from the original glue of the scraps on the front.

At morn, at noon, at night,
Thy form in fancy still I see;
In gloomy shade, in blaze of light,
My thoughts are ever turned to thee:
Bright as the stars my love shall shine
If you will be my Valentine.

The poetry and ornamentation on the inside of some of these cards is the perfect complement to the artwork on the rest of the valentine.

Take a gift, a flower from me,
Sweetest Valentine,
Simple shall its message be,
My full heart is thine.

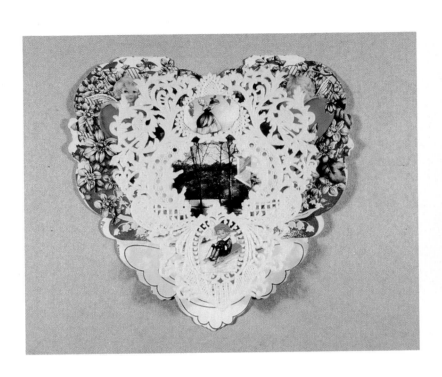

Both cards on the opposite page probably date to the early years of this century but the paper lace on the heart above, and the gold Dresden on the Maltese cross below are from an earlier time. Ca. 1900, 6" x 6" **$25+ each**

The printing on this card below dates to the 1920's, but the paper lace is lovely. Early 1900's, 6" x 8" **$20+**

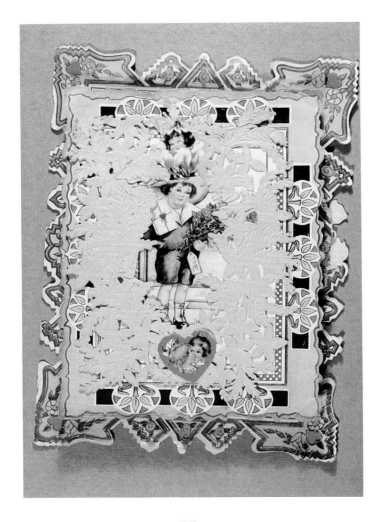

Here is a typical and gorgeous example of a German pull-out. The doves that appear on so many valentines were sacred to Aphrodite, Greek Goddess of Love. Ca. 1910, 6 1/2" x 10 1/2"   **$75+**

Pull-Outs

CHAPTER 2

Probably the greatest majority of antique valentines are the pull-outs, where children, cherubs, and bevies of doves cavort among layers of lithographed flowers on free standing diecut cards. Called "mechanical pull-outs" by manufacturers of their own time, they are not to be confused with "mechanicals", and so we shall simply call them pull-outs.

The anatomy of a pull-out is simple but ingenious. It consists of a flat piece of light weight cardboard, diecut in a delicate, lacy shape and printed in full color, with the lowest portion folded up. As this lowest part is carefully pulled down, layers of printed diecuts attached to the card by paper hinges separate from one another and appear to stand by themselves. In a few less common versions of the pull-out, both portions of the card are pulled down until they form a flat base upon which a pop-up picture composed of layered diecuts appears to be free standing.

The diecut, a piece of paper that has been cut out or stamped out mechanically, originated in Germany in the 1860's, probably in the area of Dresden, in Saxony. The word diecut is usually applied to the bits of printed paper that were called "scraps" and collected by Victorian ladies in both England and the U.S. The "scraps" were usually beautifully printed, either by chromolithography or rotogravure. Chromolithography is a process in which the effect of full color is produced by printing many colors, one over the other, from flat slabs of limestone upon which the color separations have been drawn. Rotogravure, which began in 1875, is a photographic process that actually simulates lithography but is done with metal plates on a roller press.

Rotogravure quickly replaced stone lithography, though both processes are referred to as chromolithography. The great majority of this chromolithography was done in Germany, and the resulting cards are marked "printed in Germany" or simply "Germany", while a few are marked "printed in Saxony". Valentines produced after 1930 are marked "Made in Germany".

These chromolithographed diecut scraps are ingeniously attached to the back of the card by paper hinges that probably evolved from the hinges invented by Esther Howland, and the beauty of the color printing is enhanced by strong and fine embossing.

Many pull-outs were further embellished by such additions as red cellophane or tissue paper "windows", silver or gold "Dresdens" (embossed cardboard covered with metallic foil), and little rosettes of honeycomb tissue.

All of these elements- the diecuts and the chromolithography, the embossing, the paper hinges, the gold or silver "Dresdens" and the tissue paper rosettes- all combine to create the beauty and the illusion of the most popular type of valentine produced during the first quarter of the 1900's.

This lovely lady in pink (above) awaits her valentine on this German valentine. Red honeycomb tissue fans and ramps. "Made in Germany", ca. 1930's, 5 1/2" x 10 1/2"   **$75+**

The valentine (opposite above) has a beautiful example of a gold "Dresden", as well as a purple tissue rosette. "Printed in Germany", ca. 1910, 4" x 7" **$45+**

Ths silver "Dresden" on the card (opposite below) supports a "shelf" upon which rests a scrap of pink rosebuds. Ca. 1910, 8" x 11"   **$75+**

29

The two cards on the opposite page are a pair. The pinwheels made of forget-me-nots and four leaf clovers are sun symbols, reminding us that this was once a celebration of the returning sun. "Germany", ca. 1910, 6" x 9 1/2"   **$65+ each**

The diecut background of the valentine below left has a rose colored cellophane "window" in it. Ca. 1910, 5" x 9"   **$65+**

Forget-me-nots, ferns, rosebuds, and doves adorn this valentine. Ca. 1910, 3 1/2" x 7"
$45+

Two cherubs plot to dart an innocent young lady on this valentine (opposite above). "Printed in Germany", ca. 1910-1920's, 4 1/2" x 9"   **$40+**

Another pair of cherubs on the valentine (opposite below) play behind a lacy diecut and a rosette of various shades of pink tissue. Ca. 1910-1920's, 4 1/2" x 7 1/2"   **$40+**

The very large valentine (above) contains several good luck charms including a huge horseshoe. Ca. 1920-1930's, 10" x 10 1/2"   **$65+**

The valentine message on a pull-out was usually printed on the bottom of the card, and was often quite lovely. Although these greetings are not seen when the cards are displayed, attractive greetings enhance the value of the cards.

Red hearts and red roses adorn many a valentine. Deep red roses symbolize "bashful shame". The valentine above is a good example. "Printed in Germany", ca. 1910-1920's, 5" x 7 1/2"   **$25+**

Bridges usually represent entrances to the "other world". The bridge on the valentine (opposite above) is adorned with red hearts. Ca. 1920-1930's, 3 3/4" x 7" **$25+**

The bridge on this card (opposite below) is covered with red forget-me-nots. "Printed in Germany", dated 1933, 6" x 8 1/2"   **$20+**

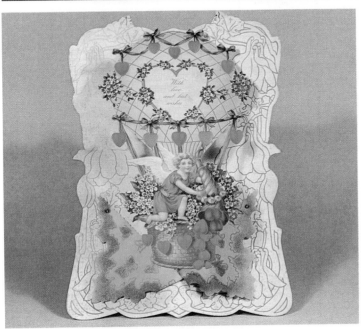

A cherub tends a rose tree, a very popular motif in antique valentines (opposite above). "Printed in Germany", ca. 1920-30's, 5" x 7"   **$35+**

The hot air balloon (opposite below) was another popular motif in valentines of the late 1800's and early 1900's. 7" x 10"   **$35+**

A garden setting of vines and trellises such as the one above right was also popular. "Printed in Germany", ca. 1920's, 4" x 7" **$25+**

Here is another garden setting (below right) with an arbor made from a birch tree. "Printed in Germany", ca. 1920's, 4" x 7"   **$25+**

A pair of cherubs entwine a heart before a windmill constructed of forget-me-nots in this valentine. Note the honeycomb rosette made of different shades of pink tissue. Ca. 1910-1920's, 4 1/2" x 9"   **$45+**

The deep blue honeycomb rosette (right) is a very unusual color. Dated 1925, 4 3/4" x 8"   **$35+**

The pale pink rosette of honeycomb tissue on the valentine (below) repeats the pink of the girl's dress. Ca. 1900-1925, 4" x 8" **$35+**

Very delicate pink honeycomb rosettes accent the incredibly delicate diecut on this valentine (below right). "Printed in Germany", ca. 1900-1925, 5 1/2" x 8"   **$45+**

41

The valentines on these two pages are among the loveliest and most ingenious of pull-outs. Made in Germany, they appear to be free standing and fully dimensional. Ca. 1900-1915, app. 5 1/2" x 7"   **$75+ each**

Here are three more fabulous examples of our favorite kind of pull-outs. The two autos (below and opposite below) are ingeniously designed to fold out with simple paper hinges not unlike those designed by Esther Howland. The auto (below) is made up of three layers, and has an original "sun roof" of honeycomb tissue. "Printed in Germany", ca. 1900-1915, 9" x 12" **$125+**

The auto (below right) is only composed of two layers, but it employs the use of perspective so brilliantly that it appears to be much deeper than it actually is. The amorous couple in the back seat is from a post card shown in the post card chapter. Ca. 1900, 8 1/2" x 6 1/2" **$95+**

The flower cart drawn by two white doves (right) is similar to those shown on the two previous pages and was "Printed in Germany". Ca. 1900-1925, 8" x 9" **$75+**

45

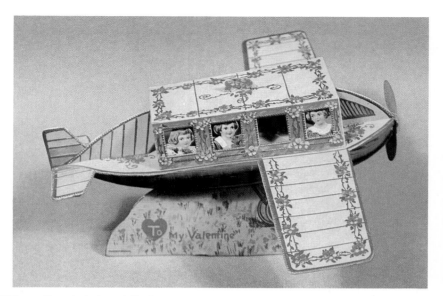

This cardboard airplane full of passengers (above) folds flat. "Printed in Germany", ca. 1920-1930's, 9" x 5"   **$85+**

This darling little sailboat (below) can also be folded flat. Ca. 1900-1925, 7 1/2" x 7 1/2" **$75+** *(River Run Antiques)*

The Viking vessel (opposite above) has its decks loaded with German diecut scraps. "Made in Germany" ca. 1930's, 9 1/2" x 10"   **$75+**

The luxury liner (opposite below) has printed red tissue sails. "Printed in Germany", ca. 1900-1915, 12" x 10"   **$150+**

Two darling cherubs (left) simply stand upon a pull-out base. Ca. 1900-1925, 4" x 4" **$15+**

A lonely cherub sits on a folded up four-leaf clover (below). Ca. 1900-1925, 6 1/2" x 4 1/2"   **$18+**

This lovely cherub (right) glides along, drawn by three white swans. Ca. 1900, 6" x 5 3/4"   **$25+**

Two tulip faeries (below right) blossom by a garden fence that pulls out to unfold. Ca. 1920-1930's, 12 1/2" x 5 1/2" **$25+**

49

This is a rare celluloid pull-out with a beautifully printed cover, left. It pulls down (below) to reveal many layers of diecut scraps. It is dated 1903, 3 1/2" x 4 1/2" **$65+**

The two small pull-outs (opposite) were "Printed in Germany" in the 1920's or 1930's. 2 1/2" x 4" **$15+ each**

The two small pull-outs (opposite below) are obviously a pair. They were also "Printed in Germany". Ca. 1910-1920, 2 1/2" x 5" **$15+ each**

51

The dirigible made of pink flowers and the mark "Made in Germany" suggest that this valentine (left) dates to the 1920's or 1930's, 7" x 4" **$25+**

The lady in pink (below) is surrounded by pink clover, denoting "industry". Ca. 1930's, 6" x 6" **$20+**

The colonial couple (opposite) is on a card that lacks detail in the embossing and the diecut. Ca. 1930's, 4" x 6" **$20+**

The valentine (opposite below) is embellished with some very fine scraps. Ca. 1930's, 5" x 7" **$20+**
(River Run Antiques)

This tiny valentine (left) was "Printed in Germany". Ca. 1910-1920's, 2 1/2" x 4 1/2" **$15+**

The cut out heart at the back of this valentine (below) had a red cellophane window, which has since been replaced. "Printed in Germany", ca. 1900-1910, 6" x 9"   **$25+**

The lovely delicate diecut valentine (opposite above) was "Made in Germany". Ca. 1930's, 3 1/2" x 6 1/2"   **$20+**

A violin of violets adorns this lovely little valentine (right). Ca. 1900-1925, 3" x 5 1/2" **$20+**

A huge white clematis, which denotes "mental beauty", accents the little pull-out (opposite below). Ca. 1930, 3" x 4 3/4"   **$20+**

55

The "Punch & Judy" puppet theatre (left) is a most unusual valentine. Ca. 1900-1925, 2" x 5"   **$35+** *(River Run Antiques)*

The pull-out valentine (below left) has a beautifully diecut background with touches of gold. Ca. 1930's, 3 1/2" x 5 1/2"   **$15+**

A cornucopia of roses crowns the artist on this little valentine (right). "Printed in Germany", ca. 1910-1920's, 2" x 3 1/2"   **$15+**

A boy and girl exchange valentines on this beautifully rendered card (below). Ca. 1930's, 3" x 4"   **$15+**

The lady on the fence (below right) is surrounded by a backdrop of four-leaf clovers. Ca. 1930's, 3 1/2" x 5 1/4"   **$15+**

The background of the valentine (above) is composed almost entirely of forget-me-nots, while the foreground is embellished with several layers of scraps. Dated 1924, 4" x 6 1/2"   **$25**

Three ladies in a basket, topped with a spray of lily-of-the-valley and accented with a pink tissue rosette, adorn this valentine of pale aqua (opposite above). Dated 1924, "Made in Germany", 3 1/2" x 6 1/2"   **$25+**

It would appear that the artist that rendered the previous valentine also rendered this one (opposite below). Ca. 1920's, 3" x 5 1/2"   **$20+**

59

A cherub plays a glockenspiel of blossoms on this little valentine (left). Dated 1924, 3" x 5 1/2"   **$15+**

Hearts dominate the decorations on this little pull-out (below) which was "Printed in Germany" Ca. 1930's, 3" x 4 3/4"   **$12+**

The two small pull-outs (right and upper right) are typical of the "cutsie-pie" cards of the 1930's that seem more to be made for children than earlier cards. "Printed in Germany", app. 3" x 5"   **$8+ each**

The gazebo on this valentine (opposite below) is a good example of a late diecut. Ca. 1920's, 4" x 6"   **$18+**

61

Both cards on this page appear to be by the same artist and publisher. "Printed in Germany", ca. 1930's, 4 1/2" x 5"   **$8+ each**

Both cards (opposite above) were "Printed in Germany" and are obviously by the same artists.   Ca. 1920-1930's, 2 1/2" x 4" **$10+ each**

Both valentines (opposite below) also seem to be by the same artist. One is dated 1933. 3" x 5" **$12+ each**

This small valentine (upper left) with its red, white, and blue background was "Printed in Germany". Ca. 1930's, 2 1/2" x 4 1/2" **$12+**

Two boys with bows and arrows take aim at a heart on this small valentine (left below). Ca. 1920-1930's, 2 1/2" x 5" **$12+**

The red, white, and green backgrounds with distinctive scrollwork indicate that these two valentines (opposite above) are .from the same series. Ca. 1920-1930's, 2 1/2" x 4 1/2" **$12+**

The red, white, and blue backgrounds on the two small valentines (opposite below) seem designed to appeal to American patriotism. Both cards were "Printed in Germany" Ca. 1930's, 2 1/2" x 5" **$12+ each**

The two cartoon characters on the valentine (opposite above) are typical of the valentines produced in the years prior to World War II. "Made in USA", ca. 1930's, 3 1/2" x 5"   **$8+**

The windmill (opposite below) is built of forget-me-nots and was "Printed in Germany". Ca. 1930's, 3 1/2" x 5"   **$8+**

A young lady holds a white cat (opposite) as a steamship looms in the distance.   Dated 1931, 4" x 7"   **$12+**

In this large valentine (above) a little girl waves a fond farewell as a plane flies overhead. "Printed in Germany", ca. 1930's, 11" x 7"   **$35+**

Here is a gorgeous example of an early honeycomb valentine that was probably made in Germany, and which is adorned with beautiful German scraps. It is self-standing and fully round. Ca. 1890-1910, 8" x 10"   **$150+**

Honeycomb Tissue

CHAPTER 3

One of the most interesting innovations to be added to the wide range of techniques used to embellish or create valentines is that of honeycomb tissue.

Honeycomb (or meshed) tissue is made when many layers of colored tissue paper are glued together at various points, in such a way that they can be opened up like an accordion. Such tissue can then be cut into a variety of shapes for stunning effects. Honeycomb tissue was probably first developed in Europe before the turn-of-the-century, and its earliest use on valentines was as the tiny rosettes used to embellish pull-outs, and to hide the paper hinges that held them together.

While honeycomb tissue may have originated in Europe, it soon began to be manufactured in the United States by Bernhard Wilmsen of Philadelphia (1903), the Paper Novelty Co. of New York, and the Beistle Co. of Shippensburg, PA (ca. 1910).

By 1913, the Paper Novelty Co. of New York had sold their stock of honeycomb tissue products to the Beistle Co. and Beistle began producing honeycomb on a major scale. By 1925 Beistle began producing valentines, along with decorations for many other holidays. More than 425 of their valentines made between 1925 and 1939 included meshed tissue, often as the main element. These designs included pull-outs, "stand-ups" with honeycomb bases and sometimes an easel at the back, "stand-ups" with honeycomb hearts or columns, "stand-ups" with an upper portion called a canopy, and "baskets". These "baskets" and many of the canopied "stand-ups" were made to open up and stand in the round, connecting to themselves with small metal tabs.

While the greatest majority of honeycomb tissue valentines are red, a few are of other colors. Some of the early German valentines are constructed of two or three sections of honeycomb, each section a different color. The earlier German honeycomb usually has smaller finer cells than the later American. Beistle honeycomb can sometimes be distinguished by the beautiful soft red to which it has faded.

This is another German fully round "stand-up" (above). The honeycomb is in three sections and two colors, and is adorned with beautiful German scraps. Ca. 1890-1910, 4" x 9" **$125+**

The "Love's Token" (opposite above) has a red honeycomb heart that unfolds when the card is opened. It has an easel on the back, and is unmarked but probably German. 1900-1925, 4" x 6 1/2" **$45+**

This is the valentine (opposite below) that started our collection. The honeycomb column supporting the Olympic flame opens to half-round but is self-standing. Ca. 1900, 5" x 6 1/2" **$55+**

This spectacular candelabra is made of three sections of honeycomb in aqua, white, and red. It is marked "Germany". Ca. 1890-1910, 8" x 15"   **$150+**

This exquisite powder blue honeycomb pitcher (opposite above) full of layers of lily-of-the-valley and forget-me-nots is German made and has a U.S. Patent number. Ca. 1900-1915, 4" x 7"   **$65+**

Incredibly delicate, this valentine (opposite below) has a pink honeycomb base and a paper lace background with touches of gold. "Printed in Germany", ca. 1920-1930's, 7" x 8"   **$45+**

73

This red honeycomb fountain (above) opens to half round with an easel back. "Made in Saxony", ca. 1920-1930's, 6" x 8"   **$35+**

This heart cut-out (opposite above) with honeycomb pedestal was made by Beistle in the mid 1930's and originally sold for 4¢. 6 1/2" x 8"   **$35+**

The two cut-out hearts (opposite below, left and right) with red honeycomb are unmarked but are probably Beistle. Ca. 1920-1930's, 3 1/2" x 4 1/2" **$25+ each**

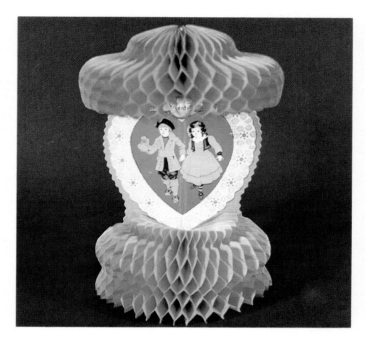

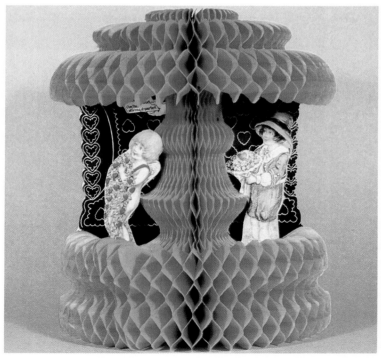

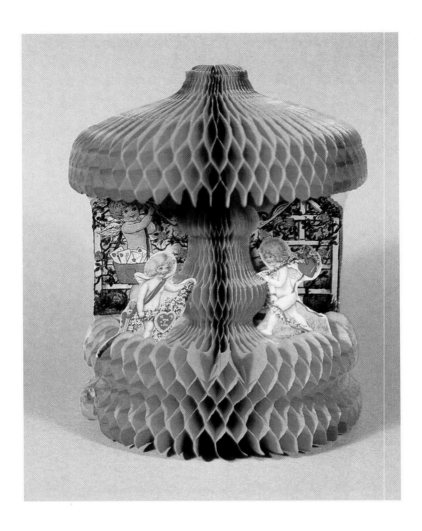

The three valentines on these pages all have canopies, and are probably all Beistle. The one with the cut-out heart (opposite above) dates to the late 1930's. 5" x 8"   **$35+**

The valentine (opposite below) has a honeycomb canopy, column, and pedestal. Ca. 1930-1937, 6" x 8"   **$40+**

The valentine (above) is marked Beistle and is embellished with scraps. Ca. 1925-1927, 6 1/2" x 8 1/2"   **$45+**

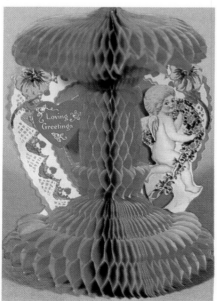
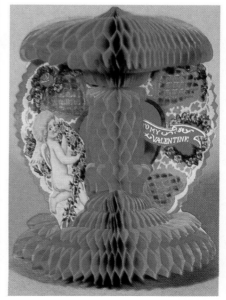

78

All of the valentines on these pages are marked "Made in U.S.A." and are undoubtedly Beistle. They have three part honeycomb and all have printed cut-out hearts, showing some variety of design. Each valentine is also embellished with a cherub or two. They open to half-round with easel backs. Those on the opposite page date from 1930 to 1937 and range in size from 4 1/2" x 5" to 6" x 9". **$35- $55+ each.**
They originally sold for 2¢ to 4¢ each.

The large valentine (above) was made from 1930-1937. 6" x 9"   **$55+**

The "Wheel of Love" (above), when spun, reveals one of many messages. This valentine is unmarked, but appeared in the Beistle catalog from 1930-1937. 6 1/2" x 9 1/2"   **$55+**

The little "basket" (opposite above) opens to full-round and the handle is printed on both sides. Marked "Beistle", ca. 1930's, 4 1/2" x 5 1/2" **$35+**

The large valentine "basket" (opposite below) is marked "Beistle". It probably had "turnover" honeycomb hearts in the basket originally. Ca. 1925, 7" x 11"   **Complete $65+**

81

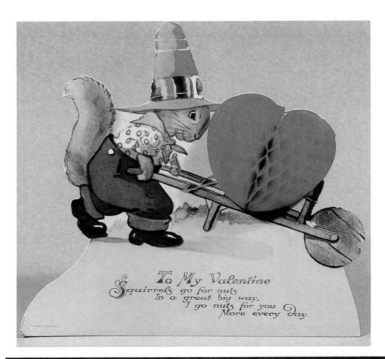

To My Valentine

Squirrels go for nuts
In a great big way,
I go nuts for you
More every Day.

The honeycomb heart being pushed by the squirrel (above left) was "Printed in Germany". Ca. 1930's, 6" x 7" **$15+**

The pink pull-out (opposite below) is here because it is more honeycomb than pull-out. Both the roof and the hood of the auto are meshed tissue. "Printed in Germany", ca. 1930, 7" x 9" **$25+**

This sailboat filled with roses (right) on a diecut cardboard easel with a red honeycomb zeppelin was "Printed in Germany" Ca. 1920-1930's, 6" x 11" **$25+**

The lovely auto filled with flowers (below) was "Printed in Germany". The red honeycomb heart is held open with a little metal tab, as is the zeppelin, and the heart (opposite). Ca. 1920's, 6 1/2" x 11" **$25+**

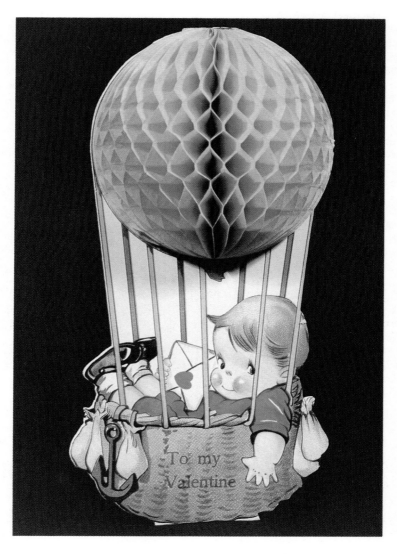

The baby in a basket with a yellow honeycomb balloon (above) is un-marked, but the artwork resembles some done for Beistle and so this val-entine may be attributed to them. Ca. 1930's, 4" x 8 1/2"   **$15+**

The unusual yellow flowers and beautifully cut honeycomb tissue on this balloon (opposite above) suggests a European origin for this little unmarked valentine. Ca. 1910, 3" x 6"   **$25+**

The red honeycomb feature on the unmarked pull-down (opposite below) is very similar to many in the Beistle catalog. Ca. 1925, 4" x 8"   **$15+**

Impatiently awaiting his date, the young man seated on the honeycomb base of this large valentine checks his watch while the lady seems occupied. Note the trousers on the railing. "Printed in Germany", ca. 1920-1930's, 6" x 10"   **$45+**

The cute couple (opposite above) appears to be by the same artist as the baby on page 84, and the valentine, marked "Made in U.S.A.", is probably Beistle. Ca. 1936, 4 3/4" x 6 1/2" **$15+**

The young couple (opposite below) are making a call on a honeycomb phone, on a card that was "Made in Germany" for the Carrington Card Co. of Chicago. Ca. 1930's, 6" x 8 1/2" **$25+**

The dancing couple on this large valentine actually do dance as their feet bounce over the honeycomb base while it is being opened. Ca. 1920's, 9" x 12"   **$55+**

The little lady on this valentine really scores as she serves an interesting honeycomb feature on this pull-out "Printed in Germany". Ca. 1930's, 6" x 8"   **$25+**

The very unusual folder above has a folded paper insert bearing a printed message. It is of heavily embossed diecut cardboard with air-brushed violets and gilded ivy. It is unmarked but probably German. Ca. 1900, 5" x 6 1/2"   **$45+**

Folders & Hangers

CHAPTER 4

The basic cards that Esther Howland purchased in Europe and brought to Worcester, MA to be embellished by her assembly line workers were simple printed folders- the forerunners of today's valentine cards. But by the time she had finished adding the paper lace, the gilded Dresdens, and the chromolithographed scraps, they were in a class by themselves.

By 1900, the paper lace valentines of the 1880's and 1890's (the height of the Victorian Era) were being replaced by the multidimensional pull-outs. But even then, the simple folders were still being produced. Now, the beautifully printed border and intricate embossing could be appreciated for its own sake, and not as the background for finely cut paper lace. Now the central design could stand on its own without being outdone by beautiful scraps.

The McLoughlin Brothers, well-known manufacturers of childrens' games at the turn-of-the-century, were among the early publishers of these beautifully printed and embossed folders. McLoughlin Bros. are better known for their sarcastic and cartoon-like cards called "vinegar valentines", which do not appeal to collectors of romantic valentines like Dan and myself, but their early romantic folders are among the loveliest.

George Whitney also produced beautifully printed and embossed folders, without the added embellishments of the 1800's, and the company that he established continued to produce distinctive valentine folders bearing the mark "Whitney Made" right into the 1940's.

Along with the folders and the pull-outs being manufactured during the early years of the 1900's, there were also (in fewer numbers) valentines called "hangers" being produced. These were usually made up of two or three chromolithographed diecut scraps attached to a silk or satin ribbon, one above the other, or sometimes two halves of a card tied together with a ribbon so that it could be hung.

While hangers had their moment and then faded into history, folders continue to be made until this day. But from the mid-1800's when Esther Howland set up her New England Valentine Co., to the late 1940's when the "Whitney Made" cards ceased to be made, the folder spanned the century that was the Golden Age of Valentines.

This beautifully printed hanger (above) is in deep rich reds on a green satin ribbon. Unmarked, it is probably German. Ca. 1900, 5" x 11"   **$45+**

Both of the valentines (opposite) are made of three printed diecuts. The one on the left has a black helebore- a poisonous plant- as the top section, but helebore, or lenten rose, is one flower that blooms in mid-February. Ca. 1900-1910, 5" x 14" **$35+ each**

All of the valentines on these two pages are with their original envelopes. Each is made up of two unmarked, but probably German, scraps.

Although several of the scraps duplicate one another, no two valentines are exactly alike. 1880-1900, app. 2 1/2" x 6"   **$25+ each**

The small heart (above) with red satin ribbon is hinged so that the cherub with the pink heart stands away from the red heart. Ca. 1910, 4" x 5"   **$15+**

The heart (below) was "Printed in Bavaria" for Ernest Nestor. Ca. 1900, 5" x 6"   **$15+**   *(River Run Antiques)*

The valentines with pink ribbons on this page are by Raphael Tuck. Ca.
1900-1910, 5" x 6"   **$15+** *(River Run Antiques)*

All of the valentines on these two pages are folders by the McLoughlin Bros. of NY. The card (above) with the little girl waving is copyrighted 1903. These cards are all beautifully embossed.

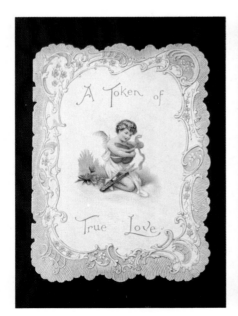

Best known for their satirical cartoons, the McLoughlin Bros. were also capable of producing beautiful romantic valentines. Ca. 1900, all 4 1/2" x 6 1/2"   **$10+ each**

The photos on the opposite page show the reverse sides of some of the folders by the McLoughlin Bros. shown on the previous page. These lovely chromolithographs seem to be a company trademark.

The beautifully embossed folder (above) with the simple chromolithographed print added in the center is dated 2/14/1896. 4 1/2" x 6"   **$15+**

The two small folders (above) are by the Carrington Card Co. of Chicago, IL.
The two below are "Whitney Made". Ca. 1930's, app. 3" x 4"   **$6+ each**

The two valentines below are the reverse sides of the two above which are unmarked but appear to be "Whitney Made". Ca. 1930's, 4" x 5"   **$8+ each**

The two valentine folders below are the reverse sides
of the two above. Ca. 1930's, 3" x 3"   **$5+ each**

Once again the two valentines (below) are the reverse sides of the two above. All are probably "Whitney Made", ca. 1930's, 4" x 4"   **$6+ each**

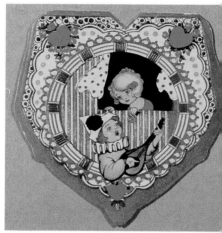

The two small shield-shaped folders (above) are by the Carrington Co., Chicago, IL. The one on the left is finely embossed. Ca. 1930's, 3" x 3 1/2"   **$5+ each**

The two valentines (below) are "Whitney Made". Ca. 1930's, 4" x 4"   **$6+ each**

Here again are two reversible valentines that are unmarked but appear to be "Whitney Made". Ca. 1930's, 4 1/2" x 4 1/2"   **$6+ each**

A cherub and a butterfly-winged faerie cavort amongst four leaf clovers- ancient symbols of the sun- on this post card touched with gold. "Printed in Germany", dated 1908. **$15+**

Post Cards

CHAPTER 5

Among the easiest valentines to find are post cards. Many of these are as lovely as their less common counterparts.

In 1846, the Penny Postage Act was passed in England, and America quickly followed. Within a few short years, holiday cards were being produced by the thousands, and among these a great percentage were valentines.

Some of the best known publishers of valentine post cards were the publishers of other kinds of cards as well. Among these are Whitney of Worchester, MA, and Raphael Tuck. Tuck in 1866 was granted the patent of Art Publisher by Queen Alexandra of Saxony (Germany), and many of his early cards bear the boast "Art Publisher to their Majesties, the King and Queen", along with a royal coat of arms. Tuck also held art competitions in quest of outstanding artists, but all of the art-work submitted became the property of Tuck's publishing company.

By the height of the post card collecting craze (1900-1915), there was a club made up of collectors of Tuck post cards, and in 1908, Tuck advertised a post card exchange register containing "the names of over 1,000 ladies and gentlemen from all parts of the world, who will exchange post cards with you".

Other very desirable publishers of valentine post cards are International Art Publishers and John Winsch. The average post card today is worth about $10, but a rare John Winsch published in the 1910's can sell for a hundred dollars or more.

One other factor that contributes to the value of a valentine post card is the condition. Generally, an unused, uncancelled post card is worth more than one that is not. However, one of the most valuable things about post cards is that if they are cancelled, they are dated (by the U.S. Government) and in this condition, while depreciated in their own intrinsic value, they are priceless as a guide to dating and understanding other valentines that are similar in style and technique.

The three post cards (opposite above) were all printed in Germany. The card in the center was published by International Art Publishers and is touched with gold. Ca. 1900-1920 **$10+ each**

Like the post cards above these (opposite below) all feature cherubs or faeries. Printed in Germany or in Saxony, two of the cards are dated 1911 and are probably published by Raphael Tuck. **$10+ each**

The two cherubs on Cupid's dart (above right) can be seen on a pull-out valentine in a previous chapter. They were published by International Art Publishers and printed in Germany. Ca. 1910 **$10+**

Cupid and companion juggling hearts was copyrighted in 1915 by John Winsch, one of the most sought after publishers of post cards. **$25+**

The lonely cherub (below right) was printed in Germany. Ca. 1910 **$10+**

The beautiful cherubs (above left) holding a heart with gold accents were printed in Germany. Ca. 1910   **$10+**

The red rose just below the heart on this valentine post card (left center) is actually satin. "Made in Austria", dated 1909   **$12+**

Cupid and a heart composed of flowers (left below) was printed in Saxony and post marked 1930.   **$10+**

The three post cards (opposite above) all feature cherubs and hearts. The clothing on the cherub on the right, like the rose on this page, is pink satin. These three post cards were printed in Germany, Saxony, and Austria, and date from 1903 to 1911.   **$10+ each**

The three post cards (opposite below) again feature cherubs and date from 1903 to 1916.   **$10+ each**

113

The six valentine post cards (left and right) are heavily embossed, and each has a velvet or satin heart with an actual photo of someone in the center. The cards were made in Germany, and may have been used by photo studios. This collection may be studio samples. Ca. 1900-1910 **$25+ each**

The two valentine post cards (far right) are probably a similar idea. The architectural motif, gilded with copper or gold, surrounds a photo of a lovely young lady holding a bouquet of flowers. Ca. 1900-1910 **$25+ each**

The five valentine post cards on the opposite page are all printed on silk which has been applied to the surface of the card. Two of the cards are the same images, printed in reverse. The amorous couple on the two cards above also appear in the rear seat of an automobile made of violets and lily-of-the-valley, a valentine in the pull-out chapter. Ca. 1900-1920 **$25+ each**

The three valentines on this page are actually embroidered on silk-like canvas and are marked "Swiss Embroidery, Made in U.S.A." The embroidered piece is sandwiched between a post card backing and an embossed cardboard frame. Ca. 1900-1920 **$25+ each**

The two post cards above are obviously a part of a series. They were printed
in Europe and have the words "post card" printed in thirteen languages! They
are beautifully accented with gold. Ca. 1900-1920   **$10+ each**

Both valentine post cards below feature a beauty of the time. The card on the
left was made in U.S.A. The one on the right was printed in Germany and
copyrighted in 1910.   **$10+ each**

The valentines on this page all feature lilacs or violets. The center card (above) is heavily embossed, glazed, and backed with another card so that the embossing does not interfere with writing. Ca. 1910 **$10+ each**

119

The three childrens' cards (left) were all printed in the U.S.A. Ca. 1920's **$5+ each**

The three valentines (opposite above) also seem to be childrens' cards. The one on the left is attributed to John Winsch. The center one is "Whitney Made". Ca. 1920's **$5+ each**

The three post cards (opposite below) are dated 1911, 1913, and 1924 respectively. **$5+ each**

Best Valentine Wishes

I love you darling fond and true
I'd like to steal a kiss from you

FOR MY VALENTINE

Let's exchange Valentines

Valentine Greetings.

To my Valentine

Caught at last!

Love's Greeting

My heart is light,
My heart is free.
My Sweetheart is bright
She'll ever love me.

121

This wonderful mechanical features a European red squirrel. Pull the string and the squirrel scurries up the tree. "Made in Germany", ca. 1930's, 3" x 7"   **$35+**

Diecuts & Mechanicals

CHAPTER 6

While the beautiful cards featured in chapter two are sometimes referred to as "mechanical pull-outs", actual mechanicals are valentines that have moving parts-valentines that DO something. Mechanicals are usually on the small side and seem to have been made to be held in one hand, while they were made to work with the other.

The ways that mechanicals work are many and varied. One way is that a part of the card is attached to a string that is threaded through the valentine. By pulling the string one way the object will move in one direction. By pulling it the other way, the opposite action will occur. The most typical method is that a part of the valentine is attached to the rest by a small steel eyelet, enabling the part to be moved back and forth. A similar method was to attach a small wheel to the back of the valentine with an eyelet. As the wheel is turned, eyes blink through openings in the valentine or a message is spelled out. Another method for causing motion was that a movable part of the valentine has a tab that projects from the valentine. When the tab is pushed or pulled the movable part is caused to rock back and forth or up and down. One of the cleverest of all mechanicals is the type in which two different images are printed in bars on a part of the valentine that is hidden behind a row of slots. By pulling a tab, one image is shown through the slots. By pushing the tab, the other image is revealed.

In contrast to mechanicals, diecuts do nothing. They are simply valentines cut out into shapes, rather than being simple rectangles. Often, they can be folded in ingenious ways to become free-standing. Diecuts represent the final stages in the period of valentines represented in this book, from the mid-1800's to about 1950. They eventually came to be sold as sheets of "pop-outs" rather than as individual valentines. These were made especially for school children who brought them to school for their teachers, who often saved them year after year, or they were dropped into a decorated box to be selected at ramdom by other children- a custom that seems to recall the ancient rites of Lupercalia.

The clown on this mechanical (opposite above) rocks back and forth revealing the valentine message in his hand. "Made in Germany", ca. 1930's, 5" x 7 1/2" **$35+**

The clown in the crepe paper collar (opposite below) moves his arm up and down and his poodle bobs its head on this valentine. "Printed in Germany", ca. 1930's, 5 1/2" x 8" **$35+**

The little puppy bewildered by a bee turns his head on this valentine (right) "Made in U.S.A." by the Rochester Lithograph Co. Ca. 1920-1930's, 5" x 7" **$25+**

These two pups (below) remind us of "Lady and the Tramp". Pull his bow and his eyes roll and tongue licks. German, ca. 1920's, 5" x 5" **$25+**

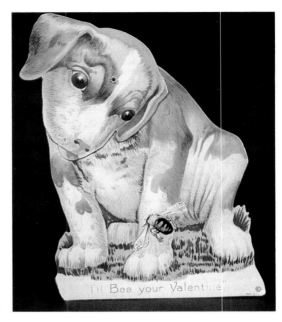

The kitten in the basket (left) rolls his eyes as the mouse bobs back and forth. "Printed in Germany", ca. 1930's, 5" x 7" **$15+**

When his tail is pulled down, this tiger (below) opens his jaws and rolls his eyes. 2 1/2" x 4" **$10+**

When a wheel is turned, the yo-yo spells L-O-V-E on this valentine (opposite above). "Printed in Germany", ca. 1930's, 6 1/2" x 9"   **$15+**

The legs on this polar bear (opposite below) can be made to gallop. "Made in Germany", ca. 1930's, 4" x 5"   **$10+**

This lady (right) answers her own questions by nodding her head. "Printed in Germany", ca. 1930's, 3" x 5"   **$5+**

The two young men (below) have movable arms. The boy (below left) was "Printed in Germany". Ca. 1930's, 3 1/2" x 5 1/2"   **$5+**

The scout (below right) was "Made in U.S.A.". Ca. 1930's   **$7+**

The little boy (opposite above) actually has three legs to help him run fast. "Made in Germany", ca. 1930's, 3 1/2" x 4"   **$7+**

The two ladies (opposite below) were "Printed in Germany". Turn their umbrellas and one blinks her eyes while the other spells a valentine message. Ca. 1930's, 2" x 5"   **$7+**

If you could look into my heart
And see what I have written there,

I'm sure you would see,
"Dear I love thee,"
And with you my heart I'll share.

I'M WIG-WAGGING "I LOVE YOU" TO MY VALENTINE

The girl in the boat (above left) with an easel back has a movable arm and scarf. Ca. 1930's, 2" x 4"   **$7+**

The girl on the back of the motorcycle (above) rocks back and forth- and isn't wearing a crash helmet. "Printed in Germany", ca. 1930's, 6 1/2" x 7   **$10+**

When this little card (opposite below) is opened, the pilot flies up to meet his lady love. Ca. 1910-1920's, 4" x 5"   **$20+**

The roof of this coupe (above) goes up and down. "Made in U.S.A.", ca. 1920-1930's, 2 1/2" x 5"   **$7+**

The spectacular baby carriage (below) is a pull-out, but the hood also goes up and down, making it more of a mechanical. Ca. 1900-1925, 5" x 5" **$45+** *(River Run Antiques)*

The boats on the valentines on this page (and the one opposite below) rock back and forth when a tab in the bushes is moved. Ca. 1930's, app. 6 1/2" x 7 1/2"   **$15+ each**

When a tab on this valentine (above) is pushed, the window shutter
opens to reveal the young lady inside. "Germany", ca. 1910-1920's,
4" x 3"   **$15+**

133

The two valentines (opposite above) have messages shown between the slats, but when the tab at the top is pulled, two silhouettes can be seen. "Made in Germany", ca. 1930's, 3" x 4 1/2"   **$10+ each**

The two children (opposite below) do nothing but roll their eyes. "Printed in Germany", ca. 1930's, 7" x 7 1/2"   **$7+**

When the wheel is turned on these two valentines (right) a message is spelled out. "Made in Germany", ca. 1935, 3 1/2" x 5 1/2"   **$7+ each**

The barrel on this embarrassed child (opposite) slides up and down. Ca. 1930's, 4" x 5 1/2"   **$7+**

The young lady on this valentine (right) cannot stop looking at herself in the mirror as her arm just goes up and down. "Carrington Co., Chicago, IL", ca. 1930-1940's, 4" x 6"   **$7+**

The young man (below) presents a pot of valentine flowers on this charming little mechanical. Ca. 1910-1920's, 2 1/2" x 5 1/2" **$15+** *(River Run Antiques)*

This lovely little girl on this valentine (left) is a diecut with an easel back. Ca. 1910-1920's, 2 1/2" x 5 1/2" **$18+** *(River Run Antiques)*

The folded diecut (below) has magnificent artwork typical of its publisher, Raphael Tuck. Ca. 1910-1920's, 8" x 8" **$15+** *(River Run Antiques)*

The tiny diecut (right) was "Printed in Germany" and is heavily embossed. It has an easel back. Dated 1919, 1 1/2" x 3 1/2" **$7+**

The beautifully painted couple on this folded diecut (below) is another stunning example of the work published by Raphael Tuck. Ca. 1910-1920's, 4" x 5 1/2" **$15+** *(River Run Antiques)*

This beautiful diecut basket of violets (opposite above) has an easel back. It is unmarked. Ca. 1920's, 5 1/2" x 5 1/2" **$10+**

This lovely limousine decked with violets (opposite below) was "Printed in Germany". Ca. 1920's, 3" x 4 1/2"   **$10+**

The beautiful cherubs on this easel backed diecut (right) includes Cupid himself. Ca. 1910-1920's, 3 1/2" x 5" **$10+**

The two beautiful children (below right) rock back and forth in this fine folded diecut. "Made in Germany", ca. 1910-1920's, 3 1/2" x 3 1/2"   **$10+**

Both valentines (opposite page) feature classic childrens' stories. On the Little Red Riding Hood valentine (opposite above) there are windows to open along the bottom of the valentine. On the Alice in Wonderland card (opposite below) there is a window in the tree. The windows open to reveal secret messages. "Made in Germany", ca. 1930's, app. 4" x 4"   **$8+**

The Cinderella scene (below) unfolds to form a somewhat self-standing dimensional valentine. "Made in Germany", ca. 1930's, 5" x 5"   **$8+**

This simple printed diecut (left) is typical of the kind children exchanged in school classrooms in the 1940's. It is probably American. Ca. 1940's, 3" x 4"   **$5+**

Both valentines (below) are also of the type children brought to school. "Made in Germany", ca. 1930's, 3" x 3 1/2"   **$5+ each**

All three of these valentines are apparently from the same series. The tabs on either side of the base fold back to make them self-standing. "Made in Germany", ca. 1920-1930's, 3 1/2" x 4" **$5+ each**

This beautifully painted valentine (left) was printed on one side of the paper, diecut, folded, and then folded again diagonally to become self-standing. Ca. 1920-1930's, 3" x 3"   **$10+**

The beautiful little valentine (below left) is diecut and folded. It also reminds us that valentines day is in February. Ca. 1930's, 3" x 4"   **$8+**

The three little valentines (opposite) all have cut-out see-thru hearts.

The one (opposite above) is unmarked, but appears to be Whitney made. Ca. 1930's, 3 1/2" x 3 1/2"   **$8+**

The two (opposite below) are refolded diagonally. All are probably American. Ca. 1930's, 3" x 3"   **$8+**

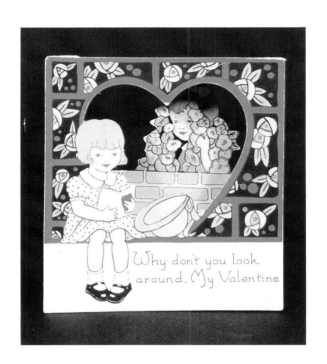

Why don't you look around, My Valentine

I'm slow, sweetheart, and shy 'tis true;
Yet Cupid loves me - why can't you?

To my Valentine

BE MY VALENTINE

PLEASE SAVE A CORNER FOR ME IN YOUR HEART

The three valentines on this page are all German. Ca. 1930's, app. 3" x 4" **$3- $5 each**

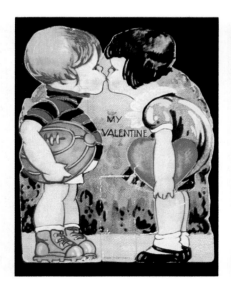

These three valentines on this page are probably all American. Ca. 1930-1940's, app. 3" x 4" **$3- $5 each**

The girl on this valentine (opposite above left) is inserted into the heart and forms an easel. Ca. 1930's, 4" x 6"   **$5+**

The little girl with the big envelope (above right) unfolds in a most ingenious way. Ca. 1930's, 3" x 4"   **$5+**

All of the other valentines on these two pages are simple diecuts and were probably printed in the U.S.A. Ca. 1930-1940's, app. 4" x 5"   **$3- $5+ each**

This catalog from the Auburn Post Card Co. unfolds and unfolds until it
forms 8 pages filled with photos. Unfortunately, it is not dated. Ca. 1910-
1920's, 8" x 10"   **$45+**

Miscellaneous

CHAPTER 7

For anyone who collects valentines, there are several related items that are also of interest because they shed light on the subject. Among these items, some of the most useful, interesting, and valuable to the collector are *catalogs*. They can tell us of the terminology used at the time the valentines were made, and they show valentines in a context. Probably most importantly, they act as a "wish list" in our eternal quest for valentines. Some of the most sought after catalogs are the Auburn Card Co. and those of the Beistle Co., as well as Dennison's Bogie Books or Party magazines.

Whoever collects valentines is also bound to be attracted to the beautiful late Victorian calling cards, made of diecut card stock and German chromolithography scraps. These scraps are often identical to those used on early pull-outs, and calling cards such as the ones shown in this chapter were often placed inside unsigned valentines.

Parties were not usually associated with Valentines Day, so party items are rare, in spite of efforts, no doubt, by the Beistle Company who made honeycomb tissue decorations for all occasions including Valentines Day. These included party hats, large hearts, and a table centerpiece. C.A. Reed Co. made crepe paper nut or candy cups and probably napkins and table covers, too. Dennisons made colored crepe papers, printed stickers and cardboard diecuts, and also gave instructions for making party decorations.

While the Valentines Day party was not a popular tradition, giving love tokens was. A love token is a gift, typically a piece of jewelry or some finery such as a handkerchief, given as a tangible reminder of one's love. We cannot assume that every piece of antique jewelry is a love token, but there are some objects made as Valentines Day gifts that can be considered love tokens.

But in the end, it is the valentine itself, given or sent, that is the most important element of Valentines Day. Sometimes, the valentine was made by hand- often a child's hand- and what it lacked in artistry it made up for with love or with intent. There is no way to put a price on these homemade valentines, but to those who give and receive them, they are priceless. For the less ambitious there were do-it-yourself kits. In the late 1940's, the years following World War II, there were kits available that combined some of the worst artwork of the period, with some of the loveliest paper lace, probably from Germany from a much earlier period. I can recall as a child using such a kit.

In 1849, Esther Howland formed the New England Valentine Company, and her assembly line workers pasted paper lace and scraps to cards. One hundred years later, the 1940's drew to a close with these do-it-yourself kits. The Golden Age of Valentines had ended.

Above is a rare celluloid card holder embellished with gold Dresdens. It was made to contain calling cards such as those on these two pages. Ca. 1880-1900's, 2" x 4"   **$65+**

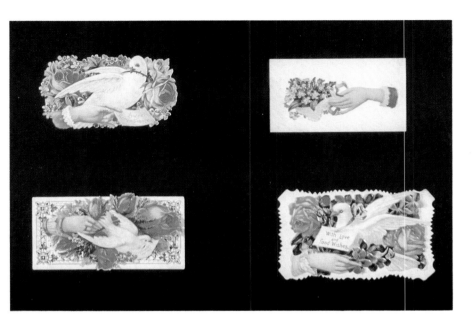

The calling cards on these two pages are all made with German chromolithographed scraps identical to those used in the manufacture of early valentines. Cards like these were sometimes placed in unsigned valentines. Ca. 1880-1900's, app. 1 1/2" x 3 1/2"   **$5- $10 each**

The gummed stickers and cardboard cut-out decorations on this page were all made by Dennison. Ca. 1920-1930's, packages 2" x 2" and 4" x 5" **$10+ per package**

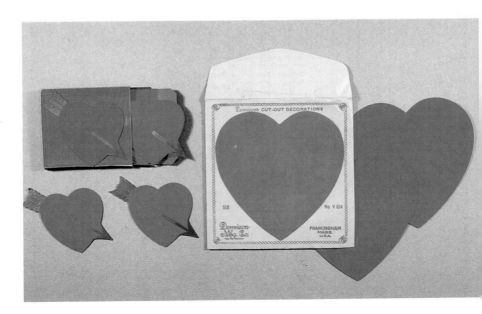

The party hats (above) are unmarked but the scraps with which they are decorated are identical to those used by the Beistle Co. on some of their honeycomb valentines. Ca. 1920-1930's, 11" across **$10+ each**

The candy baskets (below) are by C.A. Reed Co. Ca. 1930-1940's, 3" x 4" **$10+ each**

This do-it-yourself valentine kit by A-Meri-Card came with diecut hearts, folders, envelopes, gorgeous paper lace, and awful artwork.

It also came with instructions for making paper hinges just like those invented by Esther Howland! Ca. 1945, envelope 5 1/2" x 7 1/2"   **complete $45+**

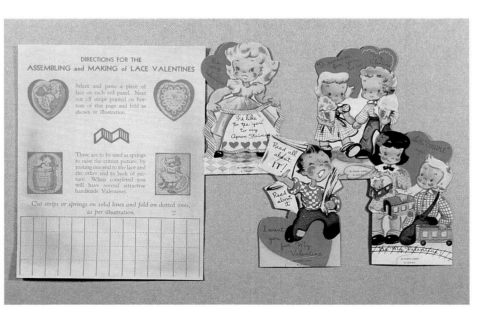

Here is a handmade love token made of cloth, cardboard, and celluloid, with handmade silk flowers and German chromolithographed scraps, in the original gift box with paper lace lining. It is marked H.H. High Quality Art Novelties. Ca. 1880-1910's, 8" x 8"   **$125+**

Below is a handmade valentine, made of wallpaper and illustrated inside with pictures from magazines of the 1940's. How can we put a price on this?